YOU'RE DOING A
GREAT JOB!

YOU'RE DOING A
GREAT JOB!

100 WAYS YOU'RE WINNING
AT PARENTING

BIZ ELLIS AND THERESA THORN

THE COUNTRYMAN PRESS
A DIVISION OF W. W. NORTON & COMPANY
INDEPENDENT PUBLISHERS SINCE 1923

For information about permission to reproduce selections from this book,
write to Permissions, The Countryman Press, 500 Fifth Avenue, New York, NY 10110

For information about special discounts for bulk purchases, please contact
W. W. Norton Special Sales at specialsales@wwnorton.com or 800-233-4830

Manufacturing by Versa Press
Book design by Nick Caruso Design
Production manager: Devon Zahn

The Countryman Press
www.countrymanpress.com

A division of W. W. Norton & Company, Inc.
500 Fifth Avenue, New York, NY 10110
www.wwnorton.com

978-1-68268-005-6

10 9 8 7 6 5 4 3 2 1

This book is dedicated to all parents everywhere.
You are not alone.

CONTENTS

INTRODUCTION

Hello! Guess what?
This book is not designed to make you feel bad
about yourself as a parent.

Can you believe it?

Look, we all know there are some people doing a bad job. That's probably not you. We also know that there are a million and a half places you can go to make yourself feel bad about your parenting. So, we're not going to be one of those places.

Here's a little story for you. Four years ago, two moms in southern California were privately having their own melt-downs because they each had a kid under 3 and it had turned out that parenting was actually about 70,000,000 times harder than they'd expected. And they were pretty sure it wasn't okay to say that out loud.

Whether through magic or desperation for human adult contact, these two moms met, became friends, and gradually revealed to one another that . . . um . . . even though they love— LOVE!—their kids . . . being a mom is harder than they imagined. This confession felt scary at the time. Scary, but good. So scary and so good that (okay . . . you're onto us . . . those two moms were us) we had a feeling we were onto something. We decided to go public with our confession.

In March 2013, the podcast *One Bad Mother* was born. Since then, we've released more than 200 episodes, covering topics from breastfeeding to sleep training to sex to friendships to judging and jealousy, and beyond. Through the podcast, we discovered that, while everyone finds some aspects of parenting hard, everyone is actually doing a totally amazing job. Parenting is difficult, and sometimes when it doesn't come easily, we assume that means we're bad at it. When we think this way, however, we tend to forget all the little ways we're actually nailing it as parents every single day. For example: Did you get up in the morning today? Great! That's hard! Did you do some stuff for your kids today? Awesome! Did you do any work or chores today? You're A-M-A-Z-I-N-G.

One of the hardest things about parenting is that it feels like nobody gives a hoot about your chaotic morning or your sick child or your flat tire or your baby who won't latch. It can make you feel so alone. What's crazy, though, is how not alone we all are. We're literally all dealing with diaper blowouts, couch stains, weird interactions with teachers, money stuff, sleep stuff, relationship stuff, and on and on. We wrote this book to remind you of all the ways you're not alone and all the ways you're doing a great job.

This book contains more than 100 entries, broken down into four chapters: Chapter 1: You're Doing a Great Job: When You're Expecting; Chapter 2: You're Doing a Great Job: With Your Baby; Chapter 3: You're Doing a Great Job: With Your Relationship; and Chapter 4: You're Doing a Great Job: With Your Toddler. Now, sit back and relax, perhaps with a favorite beverage, and allow us to overwhelm you with all the ways in which you are totally WINNING at parenting, even if you don't think you are.

YOU'RE DOING A
GREAT JOB!

CHAPTER 1

YOU'RE DOING A
GREAT JOB!
WHEN YOU'RE EXPECTING

You made the decision to become a parent. Whether it's been your heart's desire since childhood, it came to you as a "surprise!," you got the call, or you were outright tricked: Congrats! This is going to be the most amazing experience of your life and also the hardest experience of your life and guess what! Both can exist in the same space and time. You're going to be great at this—and even when you're not, remember: You don't have to post everything on Facebook!

GIVE YOURSELF SOME CREDIT

Whether you've taken a childbirth education course,
read a few pages of a parenting book, or just did
a google image search for "baby," you did SOMETHING
to prepare for this baby. Great! Now, you're ready!

The baby registry is done. You went online, or into a store, and did it. Maybe you love shopping and this was fun for you. Or maybe you just needed to get your mother-in-law/cousin/friend of a friend to stop asking you about it. (It's how they show they care.) You'll quickly realize that stores think you need A LOT OF STUFF just to get through any given day once the baby is born. And you might be turned off by the consumerism surrounding new babies. And you will doubtless endure judgments about what kind of toys and bedding and diapers you've picked out. But you did it!

So, take that, caring friends and family!

YOU SURVIVED YOUR BABY SHOWER

(and the cake shaped like a baby coming out of a vagina)!

You're figuring out where your baby will sleep!
Whether it's an "area" near the dining room table
just piled with baby sh*t or an actual bedroom in your house
with wall decals that you've painstakingly applied
only for your kid to destroy with poop or permanent marker
at a later date, you're getting your home ready for
your lucky new child! And he or she is going to love it!
Because it's all he or she will ever know.

Your baby doesn't really care what his or her
room looks like. But you do and that is absolutely okay.
Enjoy the fun of decorating it the way you want
because it makes you feel great.

YOU'RE ALLOWED
TO FEEL GREAT.

WAITING. That is A THING.
Whether you or your partner is carrying the baby,
or you and your partner are waiting/watching/staring at a
woman who's carrying your baby, or you're
looking at pictures of the baby that will one day be yours . . .
the waiting is for everyone.
It's exciting and scary and you're doing a good job.

Due dates are a real crapshoot!
Go ahead and get tickets to that concert or cancel all
your plans for those last few weeks.
If you're adopting, you may have absolutely no idea when you
get your baby. So . . . that's a real crapshoot too!

ANYWAY:
YOU'RE DOING A REALLY GOOD JOB.

It can be hard to take a deep breath and know
you are doing a good job . . .
especially when all your friends and family are telling
you these awful things that happened to them
during their birth and/or baby experiences.
Why are they doing that?
Well, good job pretending that it isn't stressing you out.

You'll get through this.

We all know your baby is going to be amazing
and you're going to nail it as a parent.
Other people's experiences do not predict or
define the experience you will have with childbirth,
adoption, surrogacy, or however else you
welcome a baby into your home
and the weeks and months that follow.

You don't feel like leaving the house sometimes
because possibly you're huge and heavy and tired of
people talking to you and touching you.
Or maybe you're consumed with worries about your
impending parenthood. Or maybe you're overwhelmed with
prepping for the next visit from the adoption agency.
Or maybe you just need to stay home
and prop your feet up on that disassembled crib while you
binge-watch *Gilmore Girls* on Netflix.
Don't worry: I think that's called "nesting!" Good job!
You're nesting!

You can't and won't know what your child will be like.
Will she have her dad's smile or a natural talent
for visual arts? Will he be a biter or a kid who thinks running
away from you in public places is fun?
Someday you'll have to—ahem, get to—enjoy all the
special qualities of your kid. For now, it's a beautiful mystery.

GOOD JOB!

PREGNANT MOMS: "LUCKY YOU!"

The first trimester!
Everything smells bad, you're tired and hungry,
everything tastes weird, everything makes you pee,
and as far as your co-workers can tell,
you've really let yourself go. Or some combination of these.
Good job getting through the most surreal and
possibly most boring (apart from the vomiting) trimester.

*The rest is easy!**

*Depends on who you ask.

The second trimester!
It's either super fun and easy OR everyone is
just constantly telling you it should be fun and easy.
"This is the best time! Enjoy all the energy!
You'll be feeling so much worse in a few weeks!"
Thanks, friends!
One way or the other, good job!
Let's remember:
You're making a person and that's awesome.

The third trimester!
People finally believe you're pregnant and,
as a result, have decided to make you feel uncomfortable
about your body in some way.
Meanwhile, your own child inside your body is
kicking you while you're down.
You're hot, you're huge, and you're hormonal.
Which means your body is doing
exactly what it's supposed to do.
You look perfect and you are powerful!
That's what they fear! You're probably a witch.

Embrace your power!

MATERNITY CLOTHES

You figured out some way to cover the
main important parts of your body that need covering
when you leave the house. Good job.

You look great.

(You actually really do.)

There's a person growing inside you;
therefore, you've almost certainly survived at least one
experience of unwanted belly touching.
Whether it was an extended family member or
someone at the dry cleaner's, your midsection unwittingly
became a disembodied subject of
squeezing/rubbing/handling.
Did you respond rudely or politely? Doesn't matter!
You did a good job getting through this
horribly awkward yet socially accepted practice
we can't seem to shake in our culture.

Are birth plans a crock of sh*t?
Heck, we don't know. But it sure feels good to make one
and walk into that hospital like,
"I know what's up! I'm informed! I'm ready for this baby!"
Whether you draft a painstakingly detailed four-page
document from scratch, copy a friend's birth plan verbatim,
or download a generic one from the Internet that,
as far as you know, looks okay . . .

It's nice to have a plan.

PREPARING FOR THE DELIVERY.

Here's an exciting fact:

Other people are going to help you have this baby!
For real! Whether you picked a doctor, a hospital, a midwife,
a doula, a birth center, or a taxi driver you'll scar for life,
you've selected a team of people who are ready to help you
have your baby. Good job! Now: Let them help you!
You don't have to actually do this all by yourself!*

*Except for the pain/contractions/breathing/pushing/etc.
You're on your own there.

ADOPTIVE PARENTS: "LUCKY YOU!"

Guess who has a baby coming next week,
or maybe in a few months, or ...
OH MY GOD YOU JUST GOT THE CALL AND YOU HAVE
A BABY COMING TOMORROW!
Or maybe he or she is a teenager or there are three
siblings between the ages of 2 and 12.
Regardless, it's about to get weird and awesome
and terrifying and amazing and totally unpredictable.
You're going to get a kid and you're going to be great.

You're enduring the seemingly never-ending
scrutiny of home visits, background checks, reference
checks, financial history checks, you know . . .
all the stuff that people who got a baby the more traditional,
"straight out of the body" way didn't have to
go through at all. Good job getting through all of that!
You deserve a sh*tload of trophies.

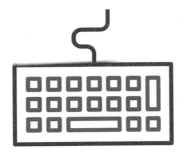

Once you've adopted your child, not only do you
get to enjoy all the ups and downs that come with parenting,
you'll apparently be in charge of teaching
every person with whom you come into contact about
the adoption process. Lucky you!
"Lesson One: Google it, asshole!"

People who have vaginal births won't be the only ones
who'll receive all sorts of inappropriate and
invasive questions and comments about how their child
entered their life. You will, too!
From "How much did your kid cost?" to "Where is he from?"
to "You're so lucky you didn't have to be pregnant.
Sometimes I wish I had just adopted," you may be subjected
to a variety of commentary you never needed to hear.
Yuck. Even when it comes from a
well-meaning place, ignorance can be a real burden that,
in this case, may fall on you.

You are doing a great job.

Here is something special.
According to the rest of the world, now that you're
adopting a child, you are officially a saint!
Or an angel! Or, possibly, the Second Coming of Christ.
Which is weird because you're just a person
who wants to be a parent, like all the other people who
want kids—and nobody's handing out sainthood
to all those vagina-birth parents.
Well, benevolent spirit or not, once you have kids,
nobody gives a sh*t—so take that praise where you can get it
and define it on your own terms.

CHAPTER 2

YOU'RE DOING A
GREAT JOB!
WITH YOUR
BABY

YOU GOT A KID!

You've acquired a kid somehow. Congratulations!
Whether a baby gestated inside you, your partner,
or a surrogate, or you made it through the
adoption process—however it went down—you did it!
You got a kid!

You chose a name for your baby.
Some people seem to like it; others don't.

WHO
CARES?

You're feeding your child! Whether it's coming
from your boobs, a bottle, a chicken leg
(each generation is different!), or some combination
of these, you're providing nutrition to your baby.
That's called keeping your baby alive!

That's a big deal!

You've gotten your kid to sleep.
How'd you do it? Nobody knows. Somehow, you got
your kid to sleep. And they slept for four hours. Keep it up
for a month, and you might stop hearing voices.

Accept that you're now going to be worried constantly
that something will kill your baby.
(I'm looking at you, electrical outlet! Household cleaning
products and previously trusted and beloved
household pets, you're on the list, too!)
Now, acknowledge that maybe it won't, because
you're f*cking awesome and you babyproofed the sh*t out
of your house! Now you can worry about something else!

You're doing an awesome job.

Somebody said something horrible to or about your perfect,
precious baby. Wow. Did that really happen?
Incredible. Take some deep breaths and don't worry,
you don't actually have to do anything.
Karma's coming to get that person . . . and it's going
to get them GOOD.

OMG OMG OMG you made a friend!!! A new friend!
A parent friend! You've still got it! You're fun!
People like you! You can make friends! And now you get to
enjoy trying to make a plan with that person, which,
considering differing work schedules,
napping schedules, kid illnesses, birthday parties,
and family obligations, will probably never happen.
If it does, you and this new friend are destined for
eternal bestiehood! If it doesn't, don't worry,
you can still periodically look at their number in your phone
and remember the time you seemed so fun
and so not creepy that another human willingly gave you
the power to contact them somewhere other than
the indoor playground!

GOOD JOB!

You found yourself on the toilet . . . with the baby.
That's okay.
This is a real achievement. You had to go, and you did.
You held and maybe even fed your baby . . .
while you sat on a toilet.

So, there's that.

You're a few months into being a parent and maybe
all things parenting aren't coming as easily as
you had expected. That's okay. It doesn't mean you
aren't a good parent. It means you're a human being.
Good job being a parent and human being.
It's okay not to enjoy this all the time.
On the other hand, if you're not enjoying any of it,
you may be suffering from postpartum depression or anxiety.
And if so, you're not alone. If you're not feeling yourself,
or something seems off, it's time to tell someone.
You are loved and you are needed and you are a priority.
You matter. It is really hard to ask for help
when you need it. Good job.

MOMMY BRAIN

No matter how insulting that phrase may be,
you did put water in the coffee grinder.
And hey, how did the ground beef wind up in the
dresser drawer? Guess what:
With no sleep and a new baby in the house,
it's a miracle that you can remember your own name!

You've been on the receiving end of
unsolicited parenting advice.
There you were, out with your kid,
minding your own business. You weren't asking
for advice, but someone gave it anyway.
It's okay to be mad when someone else
gives you unsolicited advice.
(And it's okay if, late at night, you think back
and find some of it actually helpful.
No one ever has to know.)

Sigh . . . whatever you were doing to get your baby to sleep
stopped working. A reasonable person would accept
that babies, just like adults, have changes to their sleeping
patterns, but just one night of your baby waking up
every hour has launched you back into the darkest of
places and reason is out the window.
So you googled "sleep regression" and sought support on
an Internet parenting board. Sometimes that's all you can do.

Good job.

You'll have time during your child's nap
to get your work done. Or after they go to bed.
Or while they're at daycare. But they didn't nap.
It took them three hours to go to bed.
They got sick and now your window to get something
done is gone. You used to be a person who was able
to do stuff. What have you become?
Possibly a person who can't get stuff done anymore.
That's okay. Just lower the bar and admire
how nice the view is from down there.

YOUR KID POOPED IN THE TUB AND NOBODY DIED.

Poop in the tub happens to all of us at some point.
Sometimes it feels like the end of the world.
But, when your kid pooped in the tub, it wasn't the end
of the world and nobody died. You just handled it.

Good job!

You've done something—at least one thing, at some point—
for yourself. Hey, remember taking care of yourself?

CONGRATULATIONS!

You remembered you're an actual person with needs.
You ate one *&%$!-ing meal, took one *&%$!-ing shower,
or successfully made one *&%$!-ing phone call.

All better now!

DOCTOR VISITS

Oh man, who wants to take their child somewhere
they are going to hate?

BUT, YOU DID IT!

TEETHING!

We all know there's almost nothing that can be done
to help make teething any easier, but that didn't stop you
from trying any old bullsh*t ideas suggested by
your parenting group, mother-in-law, and strangers
on the bus. Seriously, teething sucks, and
you're doing a great job.

You've forced yourself to physically detach from your kid
when you had to. You had to go to work or
get your hair done or whatever. You had to leave your
crying baby with a babysitter or daycare.
Your baby screamed and, with all your heart, mind, and body,
you wanted to go back for your baby. But, you didn't.

GOOD JOB
LEAVING YOUR BABY.

Newborns go through 6 to 12 diapers per day.
And they ain't changin' themselves!
Whether you're diapering that baby on a changing table
in the nursery, on a towel on your bed,
on the floor of a public restroom, or on your lap
in your car on the side of the road, you are doing
the quintessential parenting task literally hundreds of times.
Even if one percent of those times you've put the diaper
on backwards, you're doing a great job!

You made a mistake. You lost your way.
You didn't know something until you knew it. It felt bad.
And then: YOU FORGAVE YOURSELF.
Let's read that again: You forgave yourself.
This is a huge one. It can be the hardest thing. For some
strange reason, we think that by feeling guilty forever,
we're doing some sort of penance for our parenting mistakes.
But, that's just not true. We don't need to feel guilty.
Our kids don't benefit from it and neither do we.
Forgiveness sets us free! So, good job setting yourself free.
(But, not too free! There are plenty more mistakes
in your future for you to look forward to feeling bad about.)

You're doing an amazing job.

There you are, in something that resembles clothing. Look, you aren't sleeping—you're trying to balance a lot right now, so this just may be a time in your life when you should be happy you're remembering to wear pants at all. Good job, pants!

This comes straight from Biz's Mama and it took
Biz years to see the value in it.

"PUT A LITTLE LIPSTICK ON, BABY, YOU'LL FEEL BETTER."

Whether it's lipstick, a new top, or your favorite jeans . . .
it really might make you feel better.

Going out. It is no longer as easy as picking up your keys
and opening the door. It takes a lot of work and it
doesn't help when family members and friends don't
understand why you aren't as flexible with
your schedule anymore. It also doesn't help to try to explain
to others how date nights, after-work parties,
girls' nights out, and "no kids allowed" events will cost you a
minimum of $100 for childcare before you even
walk out your door. Also, you are tired.
Here's the deal: It's okay. This is your life now.
This is not a bad life. It is a different life. You know, a life
with a different kind of fun.

People are not going to understand why you don't want
to do the things you did before. So make up some excuses.

HERE ARE SOME

We're busy teaching the baby French
sign language tonight.

Sorry, we can't go to the movies.
We're staying home to have a ton of sex.

Too drunk already.

Take a moment and remember when you didn't have kids. That time at a restaurant when you saw a family at the next table and their kids were on iPads and you thought, "I'll never do that. That is just lazy parenting." Maybe you were unsympathetic to the co-worker who could never stay late or who got all that luxurious downtime in the bathroom stall breast pumping. Yeesh! Get out of the stall already! Then you had kids and you realized you may have been a big old jerk to all the parents you ever encountered. It's okay. There's no time limit on apologies and your penance will be the knowledge that you are being criticized by non-parents right this moment.

Circle of life!

Something's missing from your Mommy and Me groups . . . .
It's dads! For some reason, for some people, it's sinister
for a dad to be a part of these groups. Honestly?
The odds of them being there to see a boob or pick up chicks
are slim. They aren't getting any more sleep than
anyone else and just want to get out of the house, meet other
parents, and kill a few hours with their kid.

**GOOD JOB BEING WELCOMING
IF YOU ARE A MOM.**

**GOOD JOB JOINING IF
YOU ARE A DAD.**

**GOOD JOB EVERYONE FOR
NOT BEING WEIRD ABOUT IT.**

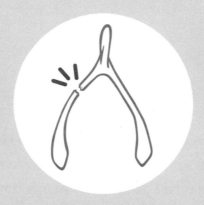

Insert here the holiday you celebrate!
What to Expect When You're Expecting left out the chapter
on the soul-crushing experience of holidays.
Between the differing family traditions that didn't seem
like a big deal till it was your child's first [insert holiday]
and the travel and the one thing that isn't really a big deal but
is now a huge deal for some unknown reason for you
(like an impossibly perfect family photo or getting time to
make something you've made every year since you
were 15), holidays may actually be the worst.
The good news is your child really will only remember
the fun and you can get through this!

If you find yourself having a holiday-induced meltdown,
sneak your phone into your pocket, claim you are having a
stomach issue, and hide in the bathroom.
If you have a baby, by all means use that baby to find
respite by announcing your baby is hungry and can
only nurse, take a bottle, drink a beer . . .
I mean eat baby food . . . someplace quiet.

Do you watch television to relax?
Then you know that you should be afraid of everything
that odds say will never happen to your child.
Isn't that the most calming thought? If you can make it
through all of the crime procedurals, the unrealistic
reality TV shows where selfishness and rudeness are
rewarded, and the most horrific . . . the local
or national news—and still allow your child to leave
the house—then that is a major win.

YOUR PARENT BRAIN IS AMAZING.
When you become a parent, you also gain a heightened sense of our vulnerability as humans. That can be overwhelming, but it can also make us more sensitive and complex people.
Additionally, it makes us good parents.
Whether you find yourself checking on your kid during the night or not allowing your toddler to play out of your sight, or if you don't blink when your kid is at the top of the monkey bars or playing with older kids because you'll step in when needed, as the parent, you *instinctually* know what your kids need.

Isn't that amazing?

(Sorry about all the other parts of your life that are falling apart around you!)

Some amount of vigilance is natural and healthy, but if you find yourself so preoccupied with things that could go wrong that you're unable to relax or enjoy your children, talk to someone about it.

POSTPARTUM ANXIETY DISORDER IS SUPER COMMON AND CAN MANIFEST ANYTIME DURING THE FIRST TWO YEARS AFTER GIVING BIRTH. HELP IS AVAILABLE.

You've accepted that it does in fact "take a village" to raise a child. You tried doing it all yourself and, while that proved your grit, strength, and—let's be honest—stubbornness, did it really work out to be the majestic image of effortlessness you thought it would be? Nope! And, you're tired! It's okay. Things are about to get a whole lot better now that you've decided to reach out to the community of humans around you and get some help.

YOU'RE WINNING!

As universal an experience as parenting can be,
there's going to be a club you're not part of.
Maybe you've got a pile of sons at home and you'll never
be part of the Moms Who Have Daughters Club.
Maybe your one-and-done only child will never be like
her friends who all seem to have siblings.
Maybe you feel surrounded by working parents while you
stay home, or stay-at-home parents while you work
full time. Maybe your child has special needs.
Maybe your child doesn't have living grandparents.
There may always be a way to interpret your circumstances
as being left out of some specific parenting experience.
(Hey, can that be its own club?)
But that's another myth. Don't let the small things divide
us when there are so many ridiculous and horrible things
that unite us! At some point, for example, we all
walk out the front door with a mystery stain on our shirt.
What is that? Feces or food? Dog urine, maybe?
Oh well, gotta get to work!

Every time you open your eyes, you're bombarded
with false images of "perfect" parenting.
From carefully curated Facebook photos to children's
catalogs and Pinterest, it can feel like everyone is
doing a better job at this than you are. Is it true?

HELL NO!

You know it! Everyone knows it!
Good job not buying into the myth. Everything off camera
is a sh*tshow. When you get that *Land of Nod* catalog
that suggests your children will be both stimulated
and well behaved if they have a beautiful storage system
in their rooms, take that catalog, turn it into a
Pinterest-perfect piñata, and beat the sh*t out of it.

You realized it's okay for you to actually enjoy
your time apart from your baby.

THAT'S SOME NEXT-LEVEL SH*T.
YOU'RE WINNING!

And you're still a great parent!

As a parent, a lot of decisions must be made when
trying to figure out what's best for your child.
It's natural to seek others' opinions, and even more natural
to question yourself, but here's the truth:
Trust your own instincts. You've got this. You're the parent.
Nobody—not your mother, not your friend—
knows better than you. Even if it feels like the whole world
is judging you, you know that a good night's sleep
is worth letting your 4-year-old hang on to his pacifier,
you know that your kid will destroy the table if she
sits with the whole family at Thanksgiving,
and you know letting your kid wear his swimsuit to school
every day for a week won't affect his chances of
holding down a job one day.

You know how sometimes it feels like
the whole world is judging your parenting decisions?
They're not.

*Nobody gives a sh*t.*

YOU DID SOMETHING THAT MADE YOU FEEL LIKE YOU.

Not parent-you, not pre-parent you. Just you. You, *now*.

That's beautiful.

Now harness that moment and do more of that.

Can we stop talking about trying to get "back"
to our "old selves"? There's nothing like pining for our
pre-kid bodies, pre-kid social lives, or pre-kid creativity
to make us feel depressed about parenthood.
Think about it. Why would you want to go back to the
person you were before? You've been there before!
You're past that now! All that stuff from before?
That's part of you, that's in you; only now, thanks to
your children, you're better, wiser, and tougher.
You're amazing. Let's move forward!

You had your first Mother's Day or Father's Day.
Was it nothing like you'd imagined it would be? Yeah,
we know. Pancakes in bed sound great until
those pancakes are served at 4 a.m. or you're sleeping
in syrup for a week. Maybe it's unclear whose
special day it is . . . yours, your mom's, or your
mother-in-law's. Maybe your partner decided Mother's Day
or Father's Day meant you should spend all day
with the kids . . . alone. Regardless, you found that this
day did not live up to the hype. Perhaps you're torn
between feeling guilty about not having fun or resentful
that you had to plan your own special day or sad
because you were given some time away from your kids
and all you want is time with them.
What is wrong with us? Nothing.
You are totally normal and you are not alone.

Do you want someone to plan you a surprise party?
Tell them. Are you unsure what you want for
Mother's Day but you know it's going to be a weird day
for you and you just need extra love and support?
Say so. Is the only thing you want in the world to be allowed
to sleep in until 8 a.m.? Ask for that. No one can read
your mind. Tell the people in your life what you want
and what you need.

You went out for milk . . . and came back afterwards.
You could have used the opportunity to run away and start
a new life! But you didn't! You came back.

GOOD JOB!
ENJOY YOUR MILK.

CHAPTER 3

YOU'RE DOING A
GREAT JOB!
WITH YOUR
RELATIONSHIP

YOU DESERVE TO BE HAPPY!

Whether you're married, cohabiting, single, separated, divorced, dating, or living a glamorous commune lifestyle, parenting babies and young kids can really do a number on your romantic life.

But love and romance are key to overall happiness and YOU DESERVE HAPPINESS—so good job working for it. Whatever your home life situation is at the moment, you're doing a good job.

WHAT'S THE BEST KIND OF ROMANCE?
Trying to conceive, trying to work around a big ol' baby bump,
trying to *reconnect* after childbirth, or trying to sneak in
some intimacy without waking one or more nearby sleeping
children? It's hard to say! We all deserve a little love in
our lives, even if it's THE MOST AWKWARD kind of love.

Congratulations . . . you did it.

PARTNERED PARENTS

You didn't choose a total jerk to have this family with.
Good job! Having a kid puts a ton of pressure on everyone.
That means you might sometimes experience anger,
confusion, or resentment toward the person with
whom you chose to make your family. But, if you think back
to that person to whom you chose to say "I do"
(or, "Sure, you can move in," or "It's okay, we don't need
a condom," or whatever), that person wasn't a total jerk!
They were pretty good. They are pretty good.
They're just tired and stressed right now, and so are you.
Neither of you are jerks!

You found a time to speak words to your partner
and listen to words coming out of your partner's mouth,
while making at least intermittent eye contact.
That's effing amazing. Great job, you guys are nailing it!

Your partner was sick and you didn't take it personally
or assume they did it on purpose. Good job!
Less to feel guilty about next time you're the one who's sick.

You and your partner were sick . . . AT THE SAME TIME!
Somehow, your family remains intact.

Gold star.

If you're sick with the stomach flu, then it's 100 percent
guaranteed that your partner will have the
stomach flu at the same time, if a partner lives in your house.
It's no one's fault. No one is trying to be sicker than you.
This is just how disease works. And it's awful.
You are *both* doing a great job. Load up with fluids, call in
the babysitters, get some rest, and try to remember
you like each other.

"I wouldn't have done it that way."
—Good job not saying that!

"What's WRONG with you?"
—Another thing you didn't say out loud,
even if you thought it.

GOOD JOB.

You didn't accuse your partner of having it easy even though, from your perspective, they do!

Good job.

Good job finding a nicer way to say, "You're just going to sit there and read a magazine?" That's a tough one!
The grass may always be greener, but remember, everyone is experiencing their own personal hell in their own way!
Respect your partner's personal hell! It probably sucks for them as much as yours sucks for you!

You remembered you and your partner are a team.
Wait—you're telling me this parenting thing
isn't a competition between my partner and me?
So, competing for who's a better parent,
who makes more money, who does more chores, and
who is more tired doesn't actually benefit our relationship?

NO KIDDING!

Okay, I guess we can just both try to do a good job
and be grateful for each other's efforts and contributions.
It's almost too easy!

You and your partner STAYED TOGETHER through the
December holidays. Congratulations.
This is a real achievement! Now, the two of you can
accomplish ANYTHING! From financial turmoil
to sexual frustration to emotional betrayal—bring it on!
You already got through the winter holidays intact
and we all know that's like the marital Olympics.

GOLD MEDALS FOR EVERYONE!

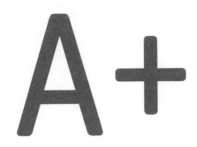

You encouraged your partner to take some time for self-care.
You little overachiever! You will be rewarded.

Your kid woke up crying while you were being intimate.
Ugh! Whether you still tried to "finish up" or you immediately
went running—naked—to your child, you deserve a merit
badge for dealing with that.

You reconnected romantically since having kids.
Maybe you locked your bedroom door for seven minutes in heaven while the kids watched a movie downstairs.
Maybe you had sex in the kitchen because your baby was asleep in your bed. Maybe you made out at the movies on your date night. Maybe you sent a sexy text message.
There are a million ways to be romantic after kids.
Turn on the Marvin Gaye and pick one!

You did something loving for your partner since having kids.
Maybe you put him to bed when he was extra
tired and handled the kids' dinner, cleanup, and bedtime.
Maybe you surprised her with a date night to go see
a movie she really wanted to see. Maybe you handled
ALL the health insurance paperwork. Maybe you left
a full tank of gas in the car. Maybe you offered a hug or a foot
rub. Maybe you brought over a glass of wine at exactly
the right moment. Maybe you make coffee
every morning. Maybe you do all the nighttime wake-ups.
These are acts of love!

Good job loving your partner!

You discovered an important key to happiness and here it is: Taking time for yourself and doing things that you want to do are: (1) good for you, (2) good for your relationship, and (3) good for your children. Isn't that freeing? Good job!

SINGLE PARENTS

Hey! If you're a single parent, that means you're
likely doing at least the bulk of this parenting stuff on your
own, so, first things first: GOOD JOB!
Whether you chose to have a child on your own or
it just worked out this way, you are amazing,
even if it doesn't always feel like it. We mean it.

You're incredible.

If you became a single parent after getting out
of a relationship that wasn't working for you: GOOD JOB.

You're awesome.

If you made the decision to have kids on your own,
you win the Confidence Award. If, by any chance, that fact
has upped the pressure that you have to be perfect
at parenting, guess what: You don't.
You get to find this as challenging as anyone else,
plus, you control the remote!

HIGH FIVES!

You didn't kill your friend with your mind when she
told you she'd been "single parenting aaaaaaall weekend"
because her partner was away.
Way to show some restraint. You're way better than her!

You went out. Preparation was involved: scheduling the date, scheduling childcare, some kind of primping—maybe you shaved? All of this is remarkable. You're amazing! Good job going out!

COMMUNE PARENTS

Quick question:
Do communes still exist, and are there people currently
raising kids in communes where everyone works
together and there's a support system in place, with
respect for one another and planet Earth?
If so, can we get in on that? Sounds pretty good.
(Unless there's Kool-Aid involved.
Or mandatory group sex—we're too tired for that.)

CHAPTER 4

YOU'RE DOING A
GREAT JOB!
WITH YOUR TODDLER

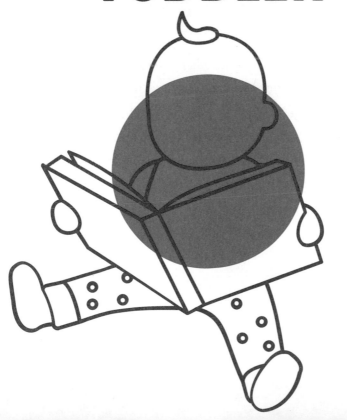

Your baby has morphed into something *different.*

A toddler!

Welcome to something wholly new from that first year
with your baby, from walking to eating real food to sleep
changes to tantrums (yours and theirs!).
You need a different kind of stamina and strength
than you did when your child was a baby,
sort of like the stamina and strength required to wrestle
a greased pig. You've got this!

You may have a runner, you may have a biter,
or you may have a climber. You may have found yourself,
pre-kids, judging other parents who seemed unable
to control their child's running away, biting, or climbing.
Oh, hilarious fate! Oh, cruel irony!
Now, you have that child, and you're realizing there's very
little to be done about it. Except hyper-vigilance and
acceptance of the fact that everything—and we mean
everything—is going to be just a little bit harder for you.
If it's any comfort, our experience suggests that
somewhere upward of 99 percent of all toddlers are either
a runner, a biter, or a climber, and some are all three!
You are not alone and you are doing a really good job.

You're most likely too busy chasing your runner/biter/climber to notice all the other parents around you who are chasing their own runners/biters/climbers. So don't beat yourself up about how you may look to everyone else because everyone else is too busy with their own kids to look at you!

So you've been talking to your darling child for months now, maybe even years, and you've gotten pretty used to being the only one with something to say. It's a little like talking to a pet, except suddenly your pet talks back and says, "sh*t." That's okay! Your baby is talking and the world needs kids with a diverse vocabulary!
Good job!

What do you do all day? We know what you do all day. Everything. You have a To-Do List a mile long, but you know what's not on it? Dressing the kids, making breakfast, cleaning up breakfast, emptying the dishwasher, doing the laundry, making lunches, cleaning up from making lunches, taking out the trash, feeding/walking the pets, making the shopping list, going to the store, unpacking the groceries, picking up toys, changing the baby again and again, restocking the diapers and wipes, picking up the kids, making dinner, cleaning up dinner, dealing with tantrums, helping with baths, getting kids ready for bed, noticing strange itching, stomachaches, eye rubbing, weird rashes, increased whining, teething, picky eating, and trying to solve mysteries. Don't forget work and trying to maintain any relationships you find valuable.

YOU. ARE. AMAZING.

Here's an idea for something to try one day:
Instead of making a To-Do List, make a Did-It List and as you
do something—even the stuff that seems trivial
because you do it every day—write it down so that
you can feel great at the end of the day.

You got your baby to stop something!
The bottle, the boob, the pacifier . . . whatever! You took away
something they love, for their own good!

Good job!

Watching your child have a total meltdown can be stressful and exhausting. It can also make you jealous. You want to stick to a routine, you need to avoid getting hungry and overtired, and sometimes you want to throw something REALLY bad and yell and scream and cry and yell some more. It's NOT FAIR!!! AHHHHHH!! No. It is not fair, but you are doing a good job being a normal human being who has limits.
Wait! Did you just empathize with your child?

Damn you, learning moment!

You swore you wouldn't allow this to happen, but your toddler is drinking as much juice as he wants, or he's using the iPad in the stroller, or you went through the drive-thru instead of cooking dinner. Whatever you said you wouldn't do back when you didn't have kids, you're doing that now. It's come to this! Oh, well.

You're doing okay!

LET'S TALK ABOUT NEGLECT FOR A MINUTE.
Neglect is a real thing that affects real kids.
But let's talk about what neglect isn't. Neglect isn't
putting your toddler in front of the television
while you work from home or study for grad school.
Neglect isn't taking a shower by yourself.
Neglect isn't leaving your baby with a sitter so
you can have a night out. None of this is neglect.
This is life and you're doing a good job.

Guess who doesn't want to eat anything
other than chicken nuggets?
(Except the skin has to be removed because it tastes
"bumpy," it has to be cut up into squares—
"EXACT SQUARES!"—and will only be eaten
if you call them "horse balls.")
Welcome to feeding toddlers! Some days you'll
give them locally grown organic veggies and free-range
chicken and other days you'll give them a naked
hot dog with a side of applesauce.
Regardless, just the fact that you're trying
means you're doing a great job.

POTTY TIME!

The diaper pail stink is starting to get to you so it's time
to start potty training! Be it pull-ups, child-led training,
or letting your kid run pantsless till they "get it,"
you can sleep stress free knowing that your kid won't be in a
diaper on their wedding night (unless it's their "thing").

GOOD JOB!

There was a time in your life when, after you'd start
your car and your favorite song would begin blaring, you'd roll
down the windows and sing your heart out into
the very face of life! It is okay if you don't get the same thrill
from "Baby Beluga." Kids' music might not make
you feel cool, but it may buy you a quiet trip to the store with
a car full of small humans . . . which sounds pretty cool to me.

Now that your baby can talk, she's capable of hurting
your feelings! Maybe she screamed, "I hate you!"
Maybe it was, "I don't want you, I want Daddy!" or "I want
Mommy!" Or maybe it was more subtle . . .
"Your hair looks funny today" or "Your voice is too loud,
I don't like your singing!" UGH. Remember, at any given time,
you are always more kind, more patient, and more
mature than your child. You're the grownup.
You can handle this. Pillows are great for muffling
your own screams when you're sad!

It was time to leave the park—the very public park—
and your 2 year-old did not want to go.
You gave him plenty of warning and tried the old
"pick one last wonderful thing to do and then we'll go!"
You promised cookies in the car and TV at home.
You did everything right to get out of that park without
a meltdown but BOOM! Meltdown.
Instead of giving into it and worrying about what all
the other people may think, you calmly picked up
that child and carried him out while he kicked and screamed.
You know what all those people thought?
That you are freaking AMAZING.

Good job.

Traveling with kids sucks . . .

F*CK
EVERYBODY
ELSE.

Your illusion of what a playdate would be has been shattered, as you and your mom friend try to maintain an adult conversation while shouting across the playground to each other while your kids do everything in their power to be interested in opposite activities. Don't worry. Parent friends really do understand and at least you just killed a few hours in your day!

They say there are seven levels of hell and we are
pretty sure three of them are made of stickers, glitter,
and sand. Each item seems like harmless fun
and is often lovingly provided to a child with thoughts of
boundless creative expression.
But remember, all that glitters isn't gold . . .
it is just glitter and will be in every cranny of your home,
car, hair, and clothing. A never-ending stream of sand
will pour from your child's shoes and pants pockets
and you will . . . yes you . . . you will be THAT parent with
stickers on your car window, in your washing machine,
or on the closet door. It does not define you.

You are going to get past this!

Guess who has an opinion about your child's birthday party? Everyone including your toddler, and your toddler has some big ideas. Whether you keep it just family, cave to the pressure to invite the entire preschool, pull off the perfect Pinterest party, or slap a pin-the-tail-on-the-donkey on the fridge and call it a day, as long as there is icing, you'll be your kid's hero.

It wasn't actually easier back then and it isn't any easier now.
Each generation of parents deserves respect.

THIS IS HARD NO MATTER WHAT.

You did it. You lied to your kids.
Maybe they are too young to tell time and you use that
to your advantage around bed time.
Maybe you told them the food or drink or candy you
don't want to share is "too spicy."
Maybe you told them their face "will stick that way,"
or you have "eyes in the back of your head,"
or that the dog has "gone to a farm upstate."
Maybe Santa Claus.
It. Is. Okay. (And we're not lying!)

God made dirt, dirt don't hurt. . . .
Or, it carries a variety of diseases. Depending on how
you look at it. So your toddler ate something awful.
Join the club! Poison control doesn't think less of you.
In fact, they're glad you called. Good job!

You just realized that your kid is not always a direct reflection of you. HOLY SH*T! This is big!
This means it's finally dawned on you that there are some things about your kid's looks, personality, interests, and behavior that just plain have nothing to do with you. They're getting influenced by genetics, their environment, other adults in their lives, and the whole wide world around them! This also means that when your kids do something horrible, it is everyone else's fault. When they do something good, it's thanks to your incredible parenting and influence.
See what we did there? Now you can finally sleep at night!

You're welcome.

Getting your toddler dressed. Here's the thing. You can either dress your kid till he's 10 and he'll look great every day, or you can teach a man to fish only to discover that fish love wearing clashing colors and backward pants. This all boils down to your personality and your kid's personality. This is the big "whatever" of parenting.

ENJOY!

The crib is gone and now your toddler won't stay in bed.
She has just discovered she is cage-less and,
like any other wild animal free from captivity, she wants
to run. Look, you may end up in her room for hours
listening to your favorite podcast on headphones because
you being there is the only way she'll stay in bed.
Or, you may end up—super-nanny-style—walking your kid
back to bed 10,000 times per night. Or, you may let her
stay up watching movies till she falls asleep.
Hey! Look at you *handling this situation*. You didn't even run
away! Whatever you have to do is the right choice and
you won't be doing it forever. Good job!

Your toddler got sick, and that's no fun. Poor baby!
This really does suck for your kid. It also sucks for you!
You've either had to miss work, cancel or
rearrange appointments, put another child in front of
the TV, and/or otherwise drop everything to care
for your sick kid. This is the real parenting championship.
Your baby is miserable and everything in your life is
disrupted, and you are managing the madness and taking
care of what needs taking care of. You are amazing.
Or at least you will be until you get sick.

You sat on your little one and forced medicine down his throat. It was one of the worst moments as a parent. Why didn't anyone tell you?
The good news is you didn't know about it because you don't remember your own parents doing it—so I bet your kid won't either. Good job keeping your child healthy!

Dentist A said to give your toddler the control
and let her brush her own teeth.
Dentist B said until your kid is 8 years old,
it's your job to make sure every tooth is brushed each night.
Your neighbor said to have them rinse with witch hazel.
Who's right? Who knows?
(J/K, we know it's not the neighbor.)
Good job if a toothbrush gets in your toddler's mouth
most nights.

Your toddler has questions about her body.
Good job answering them! You're arming your kid with good,
honest information. Your child will not be ignorant of
the wondrous workings of the human body.
And *all* other parents will thank you because your child
has educated theirs on a range of awkward subjects!
You're welcome, other parents!

CHECK YOU OUT!
Your toddler fell or got hurt, and you did something
to make her feel better. You didn't panic. You knew she hates
ice and loves *Star Wars* band aids. See?
You do know how to parent!

You're amazing!

Oh my goodness, you just got back from a party for
3 year-olds and that mom made the most amazing cake.
You still can't believe it didn't come from a store.
She is the most amazing mom ever. Logically, this means you
are the worst mom ever. Not true! You are still the
best mom ever and buying a cake at the store or making
a cake from scratch has nothing to do with it.
She didn't make the cake "at you." You didn't spend money
on a cake "at her." Cakes surprisingly have very little
to do with being a good parent. When did cake become the
bad guy? Cake is for eating! Go have fun eating cake!

NO ONE IS DOING IT *AT YOU.*

YOU LOST YOUR PATIENCE.
Naturally! Kids are famous for being simultaneously irritating,
slow, and oblivious to others.
HOW COULD YOU NOT LOSE YOUR PATIENCE
AT SOME POINT?!
The important thing is to apologize later and explain to your
kid that your bad behavior wasn't their fault
(. . . even though, sure, we kinda know they at least
had a hand in it!). Everyone will be okay—you'll remember
how sh*tty you felt and that'll help you try to be
more patient next time! That's the beautiful circle of regret!

Who knew someone so small could generate so much stuff?
We're talkin' artwork, party favors, birthday cards,
found "treasures" from playgrounds and sidewalks.
Good job throwing most of it away or, better yet, sending it
on to Grandma. Or getting a storage unit.
You're an archiving dynamo!

It's been so nice choosing the music you listen to,
the food you feed your family, the activities of the day.
Choices are great when they're yours.
That's over! Your child now has opinions. Many opinions!
And, they have the course-altering power to persuade
you with great gusto that their opinions matter.
After you take a deep breath and count to 10, you might find
yourself realizing that sometimes, they're right.
And that's okay. Congratulations: Your child has become
a real person and you've acknowledged that!
You are doing a good job.

HERE YOU ARE, READY FOR ANOTHER GO-ROUND

Through no fault of your own, you were exposed to
someone's new baby. Now you're thinking thoughts like,
"Aw, babies. It wasn't hard. It goes by so fast."
And now, here you are, ready for another go-round.

Good luck!

ACKNOWLEDGMENTS

Biz and Theresa would like to thank everyone at
The Countryman Press, especially our wonderful editor Ann Treistman,
as well as our designer Nick Caruso. We would also like to thank
our fantastic agent, Kate McKean, of Howard Morhaim Literary Agency,
who is "doing a great job" (for real).

Biz would like to thank her husband Stefan for making her the
original "One Bad Mother" shirt that made her actually feel like a cool
mom as well as for his never-ending support. I love you.
Thank you to Helen Ellis, who has never missed a show or a podcast
and who held my hand through the book process with the patience
and kindness that only a veteran writer and big sister could.
I think you are amazing. To my two perfect children, Katy Belle and
Ellis Gustaf, thank you for telling me I'm doing a good job.
I love you more than I can ever express. Finally, thank you to my parents,
Helen and Mike Ellis. Every joy and every struggle I have as a parent,
every selfish moment I want to have but give up for my children,
every moment of sheer terror at the thought of them being hurt, and
every night as I stumble blurry-eyed into bed, I am reminded of
how thankful I am for everything you have ever done and continue to
do for me. I love you.

155

Theresa would like to thank her three amazing children, without whom there would be no book or podcast as we know it! You three have given me the greatest moments of joy and learning of my life, and I look forward to everything that's still to come. I would also like to thank my husband Jesse for being so supportive of this book and the *One Bad Mother* podcast, since day one. Jesse, our relationship and our adventures in parenting were such an inspiration for this book. I'm so glad we love each other through our challenges. You're my best friend and my favorite person to do most things with, but probably especially to eat It's-Its with. Last but never least, I must thank my wonderful mom and dad, Beth and Steve Hossfeld, who taught me how to be a loving parent.

Biz and Theresa would like to thank *One Bad Mother* podcast listeners, who've given us so much love and inspiration over the last four years since we started podcasting. You are all doing an amazing job. We'd also like to thank Maximum Fun for being the incubator and home of *One Bad Mother*, as well as an awesome place to work and record the show every Monday.